## Praise for *Placebo Junkies Conspiring with the Half-Asleep*

Cohen blesses us with celebrations of family, fatherhood, friends, teachers, lovers, the sudden lost and stolen. Complete with odes to a burger-wolfing Ghandi, Dave Dravecky and David Carradine, he also tackles gravity, oxygen, trees, the big "G," coffee and wine.

In these pages Cohen, a deft (sometimes daft?) prestidigitator and linguistic escape artist who can transmute even dreck into dre, offers us a panacea of friendship and Negative Capability; it is a tree of life to those who take hold of it, and will definitely put some wing-wong in your zim-zam against the dying of the light.


Cohen's tour de force
Is required reading
For the fully baked, all those
Who have ever been in half-
Way houses or had one foot
In the agave


In it you'll find
The finest junkies and most upstanding
Sleep walkers you'll ever meet
All working together
To make us meet
Them half way


I want to get in on the act


– Loren Goodman

*For T.C.*

*In Friendship*

# Placebo Junkies
# Conspiring with the
# Half-Asleep

### Bruce Cohen

Black Lawrence Press
New York

Black Lawrence Press
www.blacklawrence.com

Executive Editor: Diane Goettel
Front cover design: Rebecca Maslen
Cover art: "A Poet At His Desk," Karen Dahood
Author photo: Cassandra Kerns
Book design: Pam Golafshar

Published 2012 by Black Lawrence Books, an imprint of Dzanc Books
Printed in the United States

Placebo Junkies

Conspiring with the

Half-Asleep

# Contents

**Section III**

Acknowledgements

For my sons—Jake, Sam & Ray

Section I

# Winter Escape Artist

To dodge the winter ennui, because even the sun's quarantined
With a nasty flu & men are not permitted to paraphrase *Post Partum*
In arguments, I bundle the kids & drive towards artificial waves,
Cranked-up eye-burning chlorine-intoxicating heat, fake palm trees
Complete with plastic coconuts, trucked-in sand, a wave machine

Orchestrated by techy introverts. Our lives are not so very different
From the twisting enclosed water slide, that dark tunnel which must be
Like birth because the first time through we scream, then the shocking
Splash & absurdly bright lights & a population already in the shallow end
Joking with one another & we feel like aliens in this pleasantly-vindictive

World. The second time through we keep our eyes wide open. Wet kids tug
My baggy swim suit begging to do it again. *Let's do it again Daddy, pretty*
*Please.* Though these are the kind of citizens I should trust, each of us sports
An elastic bracelet with a rented key on our ankles because signs warn us,
In explicit terms, to lock our valuables, that no one is responsible for loss.

There seem to be contradictions everywhere. Sandra composed a story
Called "In Fiji" where a mother decorates her drab Salvation Army
Living room as a paradise for her sniffling kids, because she suspects
Her life, their sad lives, being as they are, might only witness a sun cut out
Of construction paper & clouds made of cotton boosted from a nurse's office,

& in her story, the mother surfs on her La-Z-Boy, a fan substituting for sea
Breeze, her sweatpants rolled up for the shark-or-piranha illusion, & her kids
Trampoline from the three-legged couch to the rickety coffee table. This is what
People do who are resigned to the limitations of their lives; they vacation in
Off-season seasons & never allow their feet to ever touch that blue carpet again.

# Unofficial Life

With flea market antique tools
I constructed a bus stop shack
Along my rural route complete
With wooden benches so children would be
Weather-cozy waiting for their yellow dinosaur.
In my cupboard, flashlights pregnant
With fresh batteries, an emergency generator,
Candles as last resorts. Bad things *do*
Happen, happen to all of us, sometimes
Unforeseeably, by no fault of our own.
A young man whose car broke down
Knocked on my door. I offered him hot soup,
Use of my phone, wished him luck before
Ushering him on his complicated way.
*Here, this jacket should fit. It was*
*My son's—but he's outgrown it.*
*You never know how long the tow truck*
*Will make you wait.*
While I looked in the closet, he stole my father's
Pocket watch, a heartless little five-fingered
Discount. I wanted, really, to be responsible
For no one other than myself; often, even *that's*
Too much. Pacing the sidelines of a playing
Field, cheering the outcome of one of my sons'
Competitions, I held my palm to the sky
And queried myself, is that rain?
I turned to a stranger and asked if he too felt
A drop and looked to the sky for possible lightning.
I remember after one snowstorm another son

Said, *Hey Pops, I can't find my gloves*
*But I don't think they're lost.*
That spring, after the thaw, I discovered them:
Ten crippled fingers.
He must have taken them off for the intricate
Manipulations of his snow fort tunnel—
Some secret passageway known only to him.
Just yesterday I was mowing the autumn lawn,
Bagging the clippings, calm in a sort of meditative
State, a warmer than usual October afternoon,
The kind when you know you have hours
Of pleasant labor ahead, and even if you finish,
There's still more to do, so you are resigned
To the unfinishable, are in no particular hurry,
Acknowledging the futility of thinking your work
Will ever be done or your life will continue
Indefinitely. I was dumping the leaves
On my property's edge and saw a tall boy
Shooting hoops in our basket, and the basket,
Being adjustable, was lower than normal—
But I didn't know that then, so the boy seemed
Even taller than he was, dunking, fantasizing,
Commentating to himself his own miraculous
Last-second successes. Narrator of his own life,
He also doubled as the invisible man who controls
Time, who can stop the clock for another chance.
But something round falls short; it always does.
He will get plenty of opportunities
To sink a winning shot, or so he thinks.
This is the genetic delusion coded so masterfully:
Boys are always stealing time or wishing acceleration.

I didn't recognize that boy for an instant—then

I did; he was my youngest son, now taller

Than his brothers, handsome, muscular,

And though my own father has been underground

35 years and I rarely think of him, I imagined him

Stopping in for a late afternoon cocktail, saying

*Who's that kid with the sweet jump shot?*

Papa, that's one of your grandsons—Ray.

*And the others? What are their names?*

*Let me see a photo of your wife; I've never met her.*

The lack of someone to whom it's said

Brings bubbling anger—

*Think how the first child to exhaust his clever words*

*In a basketball argument is the one to throw the first punch.*

But it's getting late; the other boys are well on their way,

Already men. That last morning I saw you, Papa,

You missed a belt loop. I meant to tell you that.

I figured I'd say something when you got home.

# The Confidence Man's Preparation

A man schemes at his petty desk, plotting for women.
To gain intimacy, acquire fat profit, he praises falsely
Others whose habits are similar to the women he speaks to.

Anyone guilty of similar vices dismisses them as minor—
So two men can remain fast friends:
Gamblers wink across the felt & hold up their drinks to toast!

If a man fulfills his dreams, he should keep quiet, not keep accurate journals.
Hotel maids know every dark human secret but survive on minimum wages.
Before executing any scam, twirl tight the one-of-a-kind map,

Strike the wooden match with flair.
Make sure nothing in your spiel will spook or vex your target. Even
Honest men are dichotomies. The newly rich are every inch generous

While entertaining, but funnel imposter wine into the oldest, rarest bottles—
Counterfeit labels. Since their guests' palates are not sophisticated enough
To appreciate subtle nuances of age, is this a crime, harmless deception, or *favor?*

Weren't these plain people elated to be ingesting this most elegant nectar?
Didn't they later brag to close friends, rattle off the exorbitant auction prices,
Recite the bottle's lineage, describe the dusty aristocratic cellars of origin,

Repeat the colorfully poetic linguistic descriptions of the ambrosia,
Leaving not a drop of evidence to disprove the intrinsic value of what they swallowed?
Is not a man who provides such happiness to the greedy masses praised by women?

# Dead Telegram to a Dead Poet

*(For Jon "Spot" Anderson)*


*Dear Spot.* Stop. An off-the-cuff off-duty reality check: you're not sleeping it off now

Or ever again—you're slumming in a permanently recycled Night Crawler-cafeteria. Stop.

This is *Skate*, your old pal, transmitting from this sad & often difficult planet


Earth—early in the baseball season when games are postponed for snow squalls

& must be rescheduled as mid-week twin-bills during the dog days. You'd think

They'd smarten up & play opening week in warm-weather-venues. *It's still the same:*


Man's Pavlov-insane. I miss you. You'd be happy to know the Sioux City Slugs,

Our fantasy ghost-league rotisserie team, still exists, but as usual, in accordance

With your legacy, I drafted a conglomeration of Latino players with visa issues,


DUI-convicted-wife-beater farm boys barely with high school diplomas, shaky guys

Just out of rehab, roid-rage lunatics suspended for twenty-one days after flunking banned

Human hormone tests, unheralded rookies, gray-beards on their last hurrah, & the usual


Bums. Why us? It always happens to us. Maybe we bring bad omens on ourselves—

Maybe God manufactures voodoo dolls for all of us. Did I mention I miss our five a.m.

Phone calls when I was crusty eyed & you were about to pass out on the other side


Of the country, alone in the desert? Remember when we drafted Dave Dravecky

Because we thought his name euphonious Russian vodka; he developed a cancerous

Knob in his pitching arm. Who ever heard of that? He recovered, so to speak—tumor


Removed, but his arm grew so weak one game he threw a slider & it literally snapped.

The whole stadium heard the horrible crack; they showed the highlight all night

On Sports Center; his career kaput; even hot dog vendors winced & rubber-necked.

Later, his arm had to be amputated. Just our luck you said—*a pitcher with no arm*.

Now that you're on indefinite hiatus, TV screen black, I pray you channel your mojo

Into my poems. Stop—& maybe Dravecky can learn to throw with his remaining arm?

# Cooking With Deception

The way margarine charades as sweet cream butter, twins pretend to be one another
To fool their sweethearts in bed. Not to say the tryst was not worth the deception.
Not to say dishes were not, later, flung across the kitchen. Not to say flying saucers
Are not from naïve Mars where aliens could destroy our world but we could still smoke

In elevators. Walls conspire with windows, not unlike a girl who confides in her older
Brother. On normal days, the front door flings open & tiny invisible beings not of our Own
choosing scurry into the shadows; Ants Climbing Trees is a graphically named
Dish though sometimes it's fine just to let someone die. I am erasing my entire house

Except for a wall-safe whose combination I forgot but wrote down on a wall. A
Witch's brew of all the drugs & alcohol I've ever ingested soaks into my twin. This
Used to be a farm before it was converted into a greasy spoon. This used to be a funeral
Home before it was foreclosed & converted into a greasy spoon. This used to be.

I like to sprinkle real sugar on my theories, collect leather still attached to cows. Man is
So capable, yet incapable, of everything. Song birds addicted to my bird feeder whistle
Esoteric songs not associated with their lineage. They are converting to my shadow
Religion. Another dichotomy: a guy at the end of my block stabbed his second wife

In the heart with a salad fork. What *is* the proper utensil for attempted murder? I know
One eats bone marrow with one of those tiny spoons. A man on my flight got an Ordinary
nose bleed & Samaritan passengers rushed towards him insisting he tilt back his Head.
That seemed dangerous: I assumed he would swallow his own blood. Above

30,000 feet it's difficult to digest ourselves. A Chinese Emperor on his spiritual Pilgrimage
to a monastery was entertained by vegetarian Buddhist monks who Incorporated tofu to
construct an elaborate dish that tasted exactly & resembled roast duck. A famous ancient
Roman chef served an entire cow for an orgy, pit-roasted.

Apparently, the emperor & all the guests recognized the lazy chef forgot to gut the poor

Animal before cooking. The humiliated emperor was about to behead the chef when,

In mock horror, the cook unsheathed his own carving blade, sliced open the cow's belly &

out flew dozens of disoriented humming birds, & all the guests guffawed & applauded.

# Bus Tokens

Let's say you were a streetwise illiterate breastfeeding her baby
On public transportation. Let's say you had only a vague idea who
The baby's father was. Let's say you were riding that Cross Town
To apply for a topless waitress gig where the only rule was men
Were never allowed to touch. Let's say your parents were strangely
Estranged zealots; your sister, to escape, became a nun, not the dumpy,

Pasty kind you see at afternoon baseball games but the kind who take
Vows of gossip. You didn't have exact change for the bus
So some schnook with a lunch pail slipped a steel slug into the slot
For you & winked. Let's say your dream was to own your own place
But never have to trim hedges or shovel snow. It's important to keep

Dreams attainable, in the ball park. Let's say after filling out the job
Application you had a panic attack because the day-manager didn't
Even look up from his racing form. Let's say it was indeed a mistake
To drag the baby into the club, but what else could you do?
You had no one you trusted to leave him with. Let's say you only

Covered his face with your hanky so he wouldn't choke on cigarette
Smoke, so it wouldn't get into his tiny lungs. Say the other waitresses
Huddled around you & cooed how fucking cute he was. Let's say
The lullaby you sang him was a slowed down version of "Too Busy
Thinkin' 'Bout My Baby." Let's say you always sang both halves of
The duet. Let's just say I was that baby & you did the best you could.

.

# Brown Bagging It

I much preferred the universe before
Gravity was discovered, when our world
Was still flat; I've never been a big fan
Of horizons, being a loyal shoe-watcher.
I enjoyed the days when one could witness
Men commuting on flying carpets, wicker
Baskets overflowing with tiny wild tomatoes
In Aztec markets, when men & women
Were still interchangeable & we weren't
So God-dimensional, so this-religion or that.
With human cruelties chaotically amuck,
Cheating & deceit seemed A-okay because
They promoted romance in its original form.
So we drank homemade brew & laughed
Ourselves unconscious because we knew
The Black Plague was just around the corner
& every few thousand years a new Ice Age
Acquiesced us into acute agricultural adjustments.
Fishermen gutted two-thousand-pound sturgeon
& tossed the eggs, caviar, to undomesticated
Dogs & infinite lobsters littered the beaches
Of Massachusetts in the aftermath of a hurricane
& pigs were genetically fat from truffles before
We knew ourselves how delicious & if a child died
In childbirth one simply conceived another
& it was not just an aristocratic privilege to have
Leisure, superfluous time to invent art, & civilizations
Practiced human sacrifice & cannibalism was not
So taboo & reincarnation was a mathematically

Conceived hoodoo of physics & a science we still

Haven't named, not mystical hocus-pocus,

& decapitated heads bounced dizzy down

Vertigo-temple steps never blinking & how amazed

The surprised girl who first touched her tongue-tip

To sugarcane, or discovered Paleolithic French cave

Etching camouflaged with hairy spiders & crystal

Stalactites. Me, I dawdle on my esoteric park bench

& slowly digest my sad, unrefrigerated brown bag

Contents, dog-earing my paperback before heading

Head down—back to my cubicle circa *Now*

Complete with 15 paid sick days per year.

# Now Baby or Never

After an episodic half-life of highballs & shredded nerves, his hands arthritic tremors—
My poetry superhero slouches at the podium & cannot lift the water-glass to his parched
Lips, the audience polite, pretending to not notice embryonic gunk caked on the corners
Of his mouth, not to mention armpit gin-stains. Ice cubes rattling the glass seem to be
Wired to a Marshall amp—the whispering gaggle of creative writing students, attending
For extra credit, are acoustic, but the microphone samples Hendrix feedback. I wish
Most days to place the world on vibrate, squelch all conversations, switch televisions
To permanent mute. People-people, people—do you really need to express *every* random
Thought? I, for one, only repeat stuff important to me, which my wife finds particularly
Annoying. When my team suffers an injustice by the zebra-ed authorities I scream
Outrage & plead to those washed-up-ex-player-color-guys & my wife insists it is I who Am
crazy. Normal people don't shout obscenities at their flat screens she points out.
Her definition of sanity steals a nap in her secret room I can't locate. If I tilt the abstract
Family portrait just so the wall moves, but I'm afraid to go in. The students at my hero's
Book-signing are thrilled when I pick up the tab—those freeloaders swigging the last
Drops of Gigondas from a year they don't recognize as good. Even the pretty waitress,
Whom I over-tip, has a Jones for us to come back again. *Soon.* She's very clear
& specific about that. I pretend to not see the man at the next booth whose nose is
Deformed & bluish, like poor-circulation cottage cheese, or a clay duck left on a radiator,
A boxer's oxidized cauliflower ear, transplanted, very Picasso. I don't doubt his wife Once
thought him a hot potato. Wedding photos must exist that validate my theory of his
Historic beauty. Maybe love is just being very polite, pretending not to see the people
We love as they are now, ignoring how they shuffle around the house in their stained
Boxers, searching for their secret rooms, wiping, at the bistro, delicate butter-based
French Sauces from their lips, which aren't too chapped, with shirt sleeves over-starched
From the dry cleaner. Some days it takes a Herculean effort to grunt *Good morning*
before Ingesting that first cup of bitter coffee. When I am alone I want company. When
Surrounded at the after-reading party I can't wait to get home, space out in front of my
Flat screen, fondle my alphabetized wine collection, check my email, check my email...

I thought I'd be a little wiser by now, a little more of a world-participant. But my passive

Anger is a backseat driver who just won't shut up. Driving home from the reading

I'm stuck behind some idiot on his cell leaving his random thoughts on voice mail,

Oblivious to the light changing green. As a law-abiding citizen I'm obligated to blast my

Horn just as some maniac tries to beat his light, almost killing me & my wife, convincing

Himself later it was yellow, not red, Officer. At the bar my hero bummed a smoke, lit

His match, but his hand shook so asymmetrically I grabbed his wrist & guided that flame

That still exists between us to his jittery tobacco stick. Maybe life is our ability to make

Adjustments to compensate for our inadequacies & love's measured by our capacity

To overlook, make up a story if necessary, rearrange truth the way Picasso reassembled

Faces, based upon how we envision ourselves, listening intently in the human auditorium.

# To a Girl Walking By a Construction Site Ignoring the Catcalls & Wolf-Whistles

A hundred pound burlap bag of unrefined sugar

Is dropped from the skeletal second storey but nobody

Is reported killed by raw sugar—so many innocent girls

Strolling the avenues never zonked by anything so sweet.

Pretend you have only one miserable hour to live so you can finally

Tell the truth. What's a more provocative striptease than the world

Floating by? Even on the cloudiest days ultraviolet sunspots trespass

Window panes, translucent spies, influence droopy houseplants,

While minute hands hesitate, quiver with doubt, act remorseful.

You think you have your own mind but traffic signals

Are synchronized to control you into lawful speeds—

Unless you disregard those literal & metaphorical life

Red lights, that grand design to keep human traffic

Organized & moving along so nicely—so civil,

With a proper moment to pause & retouch your lipstick

Or check, in the rearview, for particles of lunch incriminating your teeth.

No one seems to pick up on most of *your* signals.

Men in hard hats scald their lips on coffee too light

& too sweet before revving up their daily jack hammering manifestos,

Spending their time constructing walls when the Taoist

General contractor has made it clear it is the empty space

Within that gives walls their value. In America you can eat

All you want or go hungry at all-you-can-eat buffets because

There's nothing you're in the mood for. New lovers take petite
Fork-tastes off each other's plates, kiss between bites;

Of course you remember what it's like to be that in love, in love
In that way! Pretend you have only a skimpy hour to live so you can spew
Any lie you want. Of all the innocents who say *I don't understand*
One type really doesn't & those who actually do say they don't,
Hording the truth. In the olden days if you simply gave a little

Sugar you'd be one of the popular girls. Most accidental deaths
Go unsolved but the media has us think otherwise. What gets
Trapped behind the fresh paint & drywall, the lies or the truth?
So you've been thinking about getting the perfect tattoo, but what?
Girls secretly cut themselves & the museum will be completed by the holidays.

# The World Haywire

During the socio-eco-race riots, street thugs & drag queens looted big
Screens & cash registers from the flaming Montgomery Ward—film at eleven.
Automatic sprinkler systems ejaculated & sirens unleashed. Brick
By piggy-brick banks dismantled. Depression-era ghosts hawked
Magritte apples & invisible pencils while checking their Blackberries.

Now suicidal day-traders hustle pomegranate-flavored vitamin water,
Day-old sushi & Co-Q 10 anti-oxidant protein bars dressed in Hare Krishna
Garb at the airports. American children are signing up for Thai sex slave
Summer camp. Carefully consider the loss of children as tax deductions
Before investing. *Past performance is no guarantee of future results.*

Cardboard damsels might give you the silent treatment for decades, stashing
Incriminating pics in their panty drawers & swabs from wrinkled shirts
Presidentially covered in sperm & unfamiliar perfume. They jerry-rig your
Brakes so they snap in a snowstorm. They only want to Ka-ching on your life.
So, under the guise of "being accommodating" you imagine staging your own

Death, like virgin snow in the shape of a foreign car in the long-term
Airport lot. In the sky, actual stars start to infiltrate imitation ones. At home,
Beds move a little farther apart. This is foreshadowing the domestic ice age—
This is the past saying *pay up bitch*—this is why zippers are always snagging
Cashmere, why bill collectors call you by your first name, why sour nurses

Giggle at the flap in the back of your hospital gown, why speeding tickets
Multiply in your glove compartment, why you're always the one being pulled
Over by a cop who contends your driver's license photo is not you, even
Though you admit your life is smoothed over with plastic surgery—how

The world is a raw deal, gravity being more than just a theory, whole

Cities shrinking into souvenir snow globes, shaken then dropped in airport

Gift shops, this is why dry cleaners let your clothes pass by on the carousel

Of garments you can't afford to pay the ransom on—why every streetlight

Is out, why they consider converting an entire generation into a single microchip.

Notice how among all the trees and buildings one tree is in fact missing.

# Dumping on the Bartender
# at the Pussy Cat Lounge

When my sons were infants I couldn't sleep—

Mesmerized, gawking into their cribs, hypnotized
By their little lungs—collapsing, inflating again.
Now they're out skirt-chasing & boozing it up
Long after I'm snoozing on the couch, or changing form—
Though my complexion is that of an aging man, in

Bar-light I'm still very much a confused boy unraveling,
Unable to resist impulsive-want—another round on my tab
For the irregulars, the men who can't ever go home
Because their house keys no longer fit their locks.
I know this may sound egocentric, but as I've aged

I'm more Gandhi-like, but secretly wolfing a cheeseburger.
I can't explain my life contradictions to part-time
Bartenders. If only life were clearer, I would have been
Less imperfect, unlike the way a drunk points at other
Drunks, blaming them for all his misfortunes & hard luck.

# Straddling the World in a Rented Car

I drove south towards Mexico, passing manikin cacti & hitchhiking serial killers.

Even the overinflated sun grew disgusted with itself, clockwatching, dreading the Duration

of its day-shift. My affections reside inside my afflictions, or the opposite—

For which dual-citizen does not have an explosive device strapped under his hobo

Outfit? My classmates voted me Most Remarkable but I did not recognize myself

At the reunion. My border town destination—Nogales, Mexico/Arizona—pony up I did

In advance for my room. A woman who did not speak English collapsed at my feet—


My Spanish only earned me a generous high school D; fortunately she began mouth-

Foaming & convulsing. Grocery bags she'd been lugging turned weightless, defying

Gravity, & her daughter—I assumed it was her daughter—having witnessed epileptic

Seizures before, knowing she wasn't vital enough to control her Madre's flailing body,

Inserted a popsicle stick into the foamy mouth so she wouldn't swallow her tongue

or bite it Clean off, barked orders at me, pleaded with wild eyes, treated me like any convenient

God. I did not pick up her panicked Spanish but do recognize human urgency anywhere.


I thought after high school I'd become the kind of man who would wise up, learn

To swallow my own tongue, or bite it when appropriate. Instead I held the disoriented

Woman in my bruising arms—prayed for an ambulance, a doctor in the crowd to step in,

But the crowd thought I knew what I was doing, viewed me as remarkable. The

Authorities, not ungratefully, pushed me aside; my audience applauded, leaving me

Suffocating in the delicious smell of garlic from a food stall that straddled my country—&

this one, south of what I know, where my afflictions co-exist with my self-affections.

Section II

# French Semester

When the red-eye we booked settles in Paris it is tomorrow morning already,

Jet-lagged, the airport lavatory coquettishly co-ed,

Five o'clock shadows & dignified damsels blot hot pink lipstick, pop rectangles

Of minty chewing gum in full toothy regalia.

I have more computer friends than flesh which says what about me?

I have more deceased friends than fresh which says what about me?

No chauffer is holding up a cardboard sign with my name carefully misspelled,

His limousine double parked, engine purring. Chaotic baggage claim—

An aftermath of French kisses vies for gypsy cabs.

I plan on composing, with tenure or without, a chockfull—

I aspire to invent wine, talk important talk, fiddle with a blues harp,

Pour heavy cream, two cubes of sugar please, into my sad coffee.

My wife swats, with grandiose disgust, flies in our sub-leased apartment kitchen

While curiously waving the good scissors she brought from home,

Scissors no one's permitted to cut with. They are—*the good scissors.*

Cranky at the Louvre, my blood sugar's taken a nosedive, I need a little bite;

I'm saturated with an overload of art for the time being.

If one of us dies in France today she can fly back to the States & be alive an extra day!

Baby, the sad thing is,

We all die anyway, on whatever side of the ocean, then the other one

Wakes annoyed that no one ground the coffee beans the night before,

& more importantly,

We will discover we are out of sugar, or without sugar,

Or expressed another way,

Sugarless.

# Convivial Pleasures

Monk Dom Perignon is said to have exclaimed, when he discovered champagne,
*I am tasting stars!* God thought temperate weather a splendid idea, that's why most
Psychopaths reside in Tucson. I bumped into Cosmo (I forget his real name) checking
Out of the flea motel—I wouldn't have recognized him if he hadn't told me he was Cosmo.
But let's not play games: God inserted a speck of Cosmo in each of us.
Apparently he woke up in the same crumpled outfit he wore the night before—
A high wire night with no net, with no parachute of skin—reeking of urine
& stagnant whiskey, achy from a bedbug infested box spring he passed out on.

Only a man like Cosmo can redefine *cosmopolitan, the Cosmos.* Joy junkie.
Whore hoarder. Combustible women limbo under the motel door, shimmy over
Ransoms, pound on windows from fire escapes. Blindfolded in a warm pool
We arm-splash through life. Someone peed in the pool. *Marco. Polo. Marco.*
The cityscape that exacerbates the landscape outside this motel is reminiscent
Of discolored bricks spray painted with talking blackbirds & pink elephants
Interrupted by a semi-official inquiry, an open-handed knock. An alarm clock
Impersonates a cigarette machine in the lobby, a medicated man spirals above

A chair in the middle of the room, half-naked, wearing an upside down silk tie,
No furniture except the bed—the smell of burnt pancakes from a diner down
The street. The fire department omniscient. You don't have to be a brain surgeon
To know we're all fugitives from our own lives, giddy on hotel beds with bank-heisted
Loot, our skin turning color, a strange shade of orange, from the time-delay exploding Dye
that makes the money un-spend-able—we are, now, entirely, dark orange.
Room Service! Dial 9 for room service—lobster steamed in fresh churned butter, my
Weight, please, in Beluga caviar (Cosmo is much thinner, as are all alter egos).

In the next room anorexic manikins pose in my favorite alluring gestures, some faux
Serious, some with fingers comically plugging orifices, smoking in bed like twenties

Starlets. *Marco. Polo.* Cosmo avoided Viet Nam & its hangover by enlisting for a hitch
In a monastery (not Perignon's) after watching every episode of *Kung Fu*, even
The confusing, trippy last season after too much acid was equitably ingested by actors
& writers alike in the hope that prime time could ease human suffering, erase
The rehearsed answers of beauty pageant contestants. Cosmo has an odd spin on
beauty: One can see snapshots of Jayne Mansfield's decapitated head, one has watched
numerous

Times *Whatever Happened to Baby Jane,* one is insane from smoke detectors with dead
Batteries. The fire engine has been summoned. One spends the majority of heart-ticks
Privately, in public, like frogs croaking, amphibians in the dark—on the high wire
Star-filled night when one kisses other humans; one is between evolutions, in the
Polliwog stage, a lonely tadpole. Researchers have isolated the gene that causes women
To turn hysterical at amusement parks. If Cosmo were to take his blind-folded eye off His
offspring next thing one knows one's drinking milk straight from the carton with
A mug shot of one's love muffin plastered above a "last seen" date. We are, in all

Actuality, kidnapped, abducted, from our own lives by aliens. One does not have to be
A genius to look through a hole in any chain link fence to witness something one
Shouldn't testify to. But when one tries to describe it, it fritters away, like champagne
Bubbles, stars traveling down a throat, like a monk scrambling to the cellar in response
To exploding bottles, an enological commotion. We are all famous in our little circles
For our mythological mishaps, our accidental discoveries, indiscretions, women tossing
Flat champagne in our faces, slamming doors open—slamming doors just for the effect,
Before emphasizing that this conversation *is. Not. Over. Motherfucker.*

# Art Therapy

I make illusionist efforts to bend the cereal spoon

With my mind, ignite birds at the bird feeder by self-effacing, flirtatious

Blinking—since we agree I am Picasso I have these morning rituals—

It seems I have a password for every thing but my own mind—

It's a strange world, *Cheri*. Car dealerships & banks counter

Intuitively close on Sundays & spirit sales are Blue-Law banned.

I rent black & white American films—women in poodle skirts


& pony tails avoiding erratic traffic, deceptive puddles,

& manhole covers. An excessive amount of bouncing goes

On in America, some of which occurs on bedsprings!

Abandoned mattresses sprout edible mushrooms in the woods behind

My zone, in the woods behind my zone a decade of discarded

Holiday tree skeletons stutter & decompose like unpracticed speeches.


Furthermore, too many passwords mushroom in my brain.

In order to get through the days I convince myself I am Picasso.

I am also a special guest-appearance of Dali in reruns

Of *To Tell The Truth*, sporting a suit two sizes too small,

Top button unbuttoned—strategic chest hairs sprouting,

Mustache overly waxed, bug eyes bugging! Windows

Are the most receptive inanimate see-through beings though


Oxygen molecules hitchhike into my lungs. Before I consume

My Cocoa Puffs, dotted with seasonal fruit—fruit, that has, a season,

I double my studio, take over the entire outside—the Cosmos.

I get more done every day when I address myself as Pablo—

For I am Picasso. At my best I am nothing but a fleshy machine

Gun libido able to impregnate inanimate objects. See how even

Dead holiday trees process oxygen & exhale. It's the first warm

Day in America & girls are sticking their bare feet out car windows,

Unleashing their pale winter cleavage on the shotgun side.

As Lao Tzu, the famous Taoist mechanic said,

*If the car breaks down, hitchhike.* On days like this, one will

Not have very long to wait. It is not now approaching at all the end

Of the world when we can assume anyone's identity we like.

# Rage

My finger is a boomerang of blame but it has a nasty splinter. Cut it out with an unsterilized boning knife. I come at the world with kitchen knives. With my forged passport I pass out karaoke microphones for family battles. I pass out rubber knives, apology-scripts and blanks of course. I hire the opinionated stenographer. I plain pass out. I install a boxing-ring bell we haggled for at a tag sale. I incorporate back-up singers who have their own unsynchronized choruses: *I just want the world to be the way it used to be when I wake up.* My business is my business and my business is failing. Even return customers now patronize the new giant chains. Don't mix this up with sprouting franchises. Each hour I mark down the merchandise till I close shop, till my business evaporates, till my gross national product is by the dumpster blooming with imperfect condoms, broken liquor bottles and milk carton children. This is the part where you think I'm a little touched (a sigh of relief you aren't me). I'm glad I'm not you either in your crumbling rooming house where the floor's moving, where plaster's flaking from the ceiling. You think people are dancing or throwing gutter balls in the apartment above but the earthquake is inside your heart and you're convinced it's only heartburn. Parked cars are rolling down the hill, emergency breaks losing interest, owners scurrying from rooming houses in their boxers or nightgowns waving documents! The automobiles seem to be giggling. Tape my mouth please. Place me in a warm bath and throw a plugged-in toaster at me and say *Catch!* I got this toaster free for opening a Christmas club account. Do they have those anymore? My family tree is a Bonsai locked in an equally miniature autumn. A limb will fall off in the next miniature storm but it seems to be a twig. What's that bug called that looks just like a twig? I smell the chlorine from the neighbor's pool which I am never invited to swim in. They are closing it up now that it is approaching autumn. They've un-inflated the smiling black plastic seal and flamingo colored flamingo. Is there any appropriate moment to grab a human by the throat, squeeze the oxygen out? I have committed suicide in so many ways I only eat oysters in months that don't contain an R but fear biting into a pearl. No one can differentiate between the intentional and accidental nails in my tire. My soul is quite threadbare too. An infinite number of galoshes are piled outside my front door. Some pairs have two left feet; some are not associated with people; some aspire to be shoes. Please get the splinter out and when you do, and when you squint and hold it up to the light bulb to see what it is, how big it is, what it's made of, explain it to me as one splinter refuses to confide in another.

# Impressionism

You've been squawking
On your cell to your girlfriend
Who's obviously on the verge
Of dumping you & the entire
World can see why.
I've been impatiently waiting
For information regarding
The weekend train schedule.
You keep lifting an index finger
To indicate it'll only be a minute
More, but after you finally hang
Up & look in my direction
The counter phone rings & you
Answer it instead of serving me.

# The Good Ship Lollipop

Walk don't run along the slippery edges of the pool & don't

Swim too soon after eating unrefrigerated tuna sandwiches.

Don't push in line—we know your life is involuntarily jackknifing

But only one person on the diving board at a time & no back flips.

Refrain from holding your siblings' heads under water for more

Than a few weeks & don't dive in the deep end with fallible

Inflatable fables if you are not a certified independent swimmer

& have a blow-up buddy. Perfect the dead man's float before

Mastering the dog paddle which might seem sort of backwards—

Counterintuitive—not to mention ominous. Respond immediately

To the life guard's whistle & return to your beach blanket

When there are shark sightings. *What!*—the pool has matured

Into an ocean! How French Noir! How progressive! Wear

Flip-flops while collecting sand dollars so you don't slice

Your feet on jagged horseshoe crabs or get stung by poisonous

Jelly fish. Evidence suggests something larger than ourselves

Does exist: a whale carcass washed ashore. Not to jump ship

Per se but who understands women who bury us alive in the sand—

Women so desperate to escape they douse themselves in kerosene

& tease themselves by striking matches before strolling out on the cliffs

& jumping without bungee cords or parachutes or functioning wings?

It was much more civilized when gals smeared sun block on

The parts of our bodies sticking out of the sand & painted lipstick on

Our protesting lips & drew an extra eye where our brains should be.

# A Rare Condition

After being poked & blood tested by the specialist who spoke *Hmmm*

In several dialects including an obscure amputee sign language, I eavesdropped

On her conferring with beleaguered foreign colleagues by the soda machine,

Whispering vowel-heavy polysyllabic antiseptic gibberish; apparently,

She'd never examined anyone with opposing thoughts in one skull before.

In the section of the country where I grew up everyone called it soda. Here they say *pop.*

I had my whole life an inkling my internal arguments were in constant conflict—

Choosing up sides in schoolyard games, my soul always the last pathetic pick.

Not that I wasn't prepared for bad news: I'm a big boy. But I anticipated something

More along the lines of tumors that grow overnight like Chia Pets, arteries clogged

With apple-smoked congealed bacon fat. Even as a child adults scolded me—

*Get with the program, be of one mind.* But I never knew which head to place

My thinking cap on. After my Siamese twin brains were separated I starting yapping

Out both sides of my mouth & was instructed to avoid other patients. I, I, I (the

Medication makes me stutter) commenced to see the world through the eyes

Of a seeing-eye dog, but after the transplant who is the real master? Naturally,

After rehab, I landed a gig as a professional dog walker whose poodles sport little

Doggy sweaters that match their owners', like those dog-humans who wear their silly

Brains outside their heads. I vacationed in every emergency room east of myself

& sat naked for weekly eternities on icy stainless steel tables sketching the diagrams

Of the color-coded digestive system, or taking a peek at previous patients' charts.

Staring at the medical scale, I could be the carnival guy who professes to guess

Your actual weight within two pounds & awards you stuffed cartoony-colored animals

If I'm wrong. Hearing the radiator clank I could be chained to a radiator composing

Fortune cookie wisdom. Waiting for the new doctor I could be the faceless

Who squidgy-cleans your windshield when you stop for a red light. (You did stop

At the red light didn't you, even though it was 2 a.m. & maybe you had a little too

Much to drink.) My shirt size is so evolving I buy irregulars. I am the dull thought

Of any man who's been laid off for a decade but leaves the house each morning

With an unstoppable grin as though nothing's wrong & pushes his pen so deeply

Into the racing forms at the track the sheet rips. His wife isn't *with the program*;

She's only cultivated one brain; so they have no children. Walking home, I am

Confused by the emaciated girl in the picture window who looks more like a mannequin

Than the mannequin she undresses. Oh, I can still talk to myself. My reflection

Is almost always in the mirror, shellacked with radioactive radio waves rationed

In the most advantageous ratio of life & living. I am my own disease I am the cure.

# The Room

When certain people enter a room the room disappears.

When particular types enter a room everyone else disappears.

After a night of hard drinking you flop onto your bed,

Still costumed in evening garb, & the room spins unmercifully.

When an architect designs a room he sketches parallel lines

Going somewhere only he sees, undetectable infinite rooms within rooms.

When an arborist plants a tree in a room he imagines the dendrochronology,

The way any future ring can be traced back to this exact moment.

When the astronomer explores the universe through his telescope he witnesses

How rooms hide themselves within other rooms. When a painter

Brushstrokes the room he sees variations of colorlessness unrecognizable

To the average Joe. Sometimes you enter a room & a trickster has rearranged

The furniture while you were sleeping & you place a full tumbler of red wine

In the air where a table once stood & in no time at all you are on your hands

& knees sopping up the stain with a shirt that still had a few good years left in it.

When a dentist is late to the examination room he mumbles small-talk but you can't

Respond due to the sterilized utensils infiltrating your mouth & when a substitute

Prances into a room the private conversations of students, who are up to no good,

Hush & when the fuzz storms the room we flatten our hands against

The walls & flush illegal substances down toilets & toss contraband

Under couch cushions & make up alibis that might sound believable

Only to anyone on the inside & when the cell door creaks open because

The lock was faulty, the latch unstable, he decides not to escape,

& someone is pounding from the other side of the wall because

The music's too damn loud & someone has an empty hotel glass cupped

On the other side of the wall with her ear pressed to the glass

Trying to overhear the clandestine sex or uncover evidence of a secret plot

& when a breeze dissects the room through an open window the tulips

Sway just as if they weren't violently yanked from their orderly beds

& a finch suicides into the shut window but no one mourns & when

A hysterical girl divides the room, screaming for her brother, you know

There's trouble afoot & the neighborhood will be buzzing & miners

Trapped underground, on their fourth day without food, begin to talk

About God in a way that men do who, though they know death is inevitable,

Recognize how it shows its face by candlelight & how helpless we all are.

You might enter any or all of these rooms but part of you is never permitted

To leave so you stand in the hallway trying to decide whether or not to go in.

# Divine Wow:

Select one isolated cloud.

Spy it your entire life, like a personal impersonator.

The fish in the diner's aquarium blink twice for yes.

God sends cryptic messages, only to me, on these stained menus

After the 24-hour diner closes.

During my meal I express to my imaginary waitress the free water tastes

Like it's smuggled from an aquarium; I detect a hint of algae.

I concede doughnuts are three-dimensional, but why

Are waitresses smuggling new bacteria out of this world in their tips?

What if God were common lint?

I'll leave the car running on the approach to the bridge.

No lousy tipper, as the wind kicks up I peel off C-notes & Sawbucks & Fins

& lonely George Washingtons & let them migrate off the bridge.

I did not fathom the full extent of myself until I reached the very top of the bridge.

A disorderly V of geese broke rank in complex denominations—

All prime numbers. One feather less than prime.

Select one fish from the aquarium & wink. The river below is a replica

Of an aquarium whose H2O is vaguely three-dimensional,

Where I can smuggle exotic fish out of this glass world.

Cumulous clouds are God's spies. My life has been lived badly already—

By a stunt man, an extra. I am my own twin—the problem & solution.

I have seen this movie already. Both the original & the remake.

Who among us is not an abstract number composed of a whispering

Linear math wind? Who is not a regular guy slumping in a diner slurping coffee?


I wanted only to have a repartee of driver's licenses representing the dozens of disparate

States all with capital letters, lots of aliases,

Blow up sex dolls & hitchhikers buried along the Interstates,


Like a sequestered jury brushing its collective teeth, sharing one toothbrush.

Illogical to think there is one God, still, or still no God.

In the evening I scrape together change from sofa cushions & glove compartments


In the humdrum. Or is it conundrum?

God's a stunt man, a stand-in, who takes my place when I'm living in my elsewhere—

A little hung over from innuendos & the brittle silence after,


Coming to grips with coffee aromas diligently regressing back

Into their beans of embryonic origin, will I forget & simply drive away

Or simply drive away?

# The Czar of Hartford

For breakfast I engaged in a blinking contest with my fried eggs;
By afternoon I was playing chicken with commuter trains that acted
Like homing pigeons back to Hartford; tonight I'll race through

The Projects flashing my high beams. People seem to arrive in two
Varieties: all talk or all ears. When young no one has dibs on the world—
In the blink of an eye pigeon-populated properties are boarded up,

But I hold out real hope of being alive again sometime when my ticker
& brain will be properly synchronized so that the wind won't play
Keep-away with a hat that keeps getting exchanged from an after-Christmas sale.

We rarely admit how **For Rent** we humans are.

Insurance agents are leaping out office windows at exactly five minutes
Before five, their parachutes made of obsolete policies. Shy men flap
Their arms thinking they might grow feathers & fly a little before they crash.

Last night I purchased an exquisite vintage port that requires a good
Two decades of cellaring. Perhaps, someday maybe, my sons will
Toast me. Maybe God is even crueler than we think & has simply

Dangled us in this isolating world—as the live bait.
The easiest thing for any man to do is counterfeit his own currency—
The hardest part being brash enough to circulate it in public.

# Slug Nation

Into the various living room fabrics he melts,
Some man-made, some natural, remote in hand.
Suicide's gotten a miserable rap—
It needs a new PR front man.

At this era of his life the clock's minute
Hand is AWOL, the hour hand frozen.
He recollects time in floating chunks
Of grief-years, a stack of Marvel comics

Camouflaging the coffee table,
Ornaments of empty airplane vodka bottles
In virtually every nook and cranny,
The giant flat widescreen purchased

With cash from his NEA Grant
Not yet hooked up for Hi Def
But blaring at all hours,
Loud, really loud,

And his pristine vintage video porn collection.
His hearing along with most other functions
Is on sabbatical; sometimes he walks
Into a room with no idea what he went there for.

He opens the refrigerator not hungry,
Not not-hungry, at least not for the expired
Faux-French mustard. Car keys are God
Knows where and mostly the phone's off the hook

Not always on purpose,

Tipped over by The Dog.

He loved what's-his-name, The Dog.

The evening before he decided


To digest this conglomeration of trippy pills,

This tie-dye assortment of uppers, downers,

Sideways-ers, washed down by, what else?

Vodka, meticulously in nineteenth century script


He wrote out all his bills, securing

Them with a fat blue rubber band,

Slipped them into the metallic blue contraption

So his solitary heir would not have to


Bother with such triviality this month.

He opened the mailbox three times

To make sure the bills were properly

Swallowed too. He should have transitioned


To beer when he had the chance

Because his esophagus was bleeding

Raw from, you guessed it, the euphonious

Gentle stream of vodka. If more time existed.


*If more time existed.* A mime is chasing

Butterflies, trying to capture them

In his bare hands without killing them

While his world is reduced inside a glass box.

*His* world mostly is shrinking and growing
More deprived of oxygen in the talking glass box.
Sometimes he calls it The Television,
Which isn't wired yet for High Definition.

Yes he is painful to watch, eating sushi,
Fumbling for the first time with chopsticks
Drunk on low-end Saki, very drunk, very-very drunk.
The powers that be (not Buddha) ended

The fishing season earlier than usual
This year. Men, on their looked-forward-to
Labor Day week-end escape, their vamoose
From their respective glass-box lives,

Being exquisite rule followers
And ecologically minded monks,
Dropped their lines into the stream without bait,
Without hooks even, sat in silent meditations,

Gulped their delicious beers and hoped
For the stupidest fish in the universe
To mosey along playing hooky from its pals.
Ultimately the fish don't matter.

Ultimately nobody matters. This is how
He views the masses. Paint eyeballs on your
Eyelids and nobody will be the wiser. Blink
And the most vibrant colors of autumn

Could be missed. That is the shame.

Go ahead. Dare me to jump he says.

He will. He swears to me he will.

But take a video. It lasts longer.

Section III

# Rediscovering Gravity

I was killing time wandering through my computer clicking stuff.

Someone was pounding on my door and said they were the police

But I knew it wasn't the police the police just kick your door in.

I watch enough Law and Order so I didn't even answer the door.

I was reading a bunch of horoscopes till I found one that suited me.

At this point in my life, approaching the age my father died,

I figure I'm playing with house money. My father was a big

Perry Mason fan and sat on the floor in front of the coffee table

Shelling Indian nuts and drinking homemade vanilla egg creams.

You think there's more to life? This was in the days before

Remotes and I was his channel changing slave and TV guide reader.

If you knew what a bad-ass tough guy I am you would be even

More shocked over the revelation that I purchased, on-line have you,

A Carpenters' CD, embarrassed to buy it in person, this very soft,

Soft porn, getting a hard-on from the corny songs. But it's not

All candy and roses and teddy bears; Karen was anorexic or bulimic

Which makes me a fan. I needed fresh air so sat under an apple tree

A la Isaac Newton. The idea-apple rotted, conked me on the noggin

And my fingers singed from smoking the cigarettes of despair down

To the very filters, to the roaches, and women from my past were almost

Angels now, but sitting in the tallest limbs with blow guns and poisonous

Darts but showing restraint. They'd spit but not really spit down

On me. It was more of a puckering like a kiss and they let the saliva

Simply drop from their lips. They had been snacking on Oreos

And very dark inky grape juice and had not bothered to brush their teeth.

When their spit landed on my head I thought it was the blood

Of a squashed bug I had killed though I didn't remember killing any.

# A Case In Point

Sometimes I'm the half-loaded, three-day stubble man—
Conspiring with the half-asleep.


If I weren't, it might be so damn dawn before I even know it.


The train's illusion between the penultimate car
& the schizophrenic caboose
Seems unnaturally loose in this absinthe dark,


Peppering my windows with microscopic pebbles, Morse code for
*My woman never made it home last night—*


Or the night before,
Like exchanging a shirt after Christmas but for the exact same shirt,


Marked down, reductions taken at the register.
At this between-hour, all shirt colors are milky-green chameleons,


Scribbled names & equivalency diploma applications show up inside matchbooks,
Tossed out passenger windows of boosted vintage Thunderbirds
Or left on beer-sticky tables in biker bars
With accidentally unplugged juke boxes & no visible waitresses to speak of.


In the real dark, insects scurry in sugar bowls, meticulously
Calculating the exigent grains of sweetness.


I really want to *really* read the hand-shaky lipstick message you scribbled
On the bathroom mirror,
So begins my frenetic room to room treasure hunt—

By dawn, I pounce

Into the stolen car, my Americanized jalopy that may need a jump,

(& nobody seems to carry cables anymore)—


Adjust the rear view mirror for a better view of the man I was &


Notice a dehydrating dab of shaving cream

Plugging my ear & tenderly remember you as the tiny bubbles pop.

# City Tree

Behind the steering wheel of a tire-heisted, semi-torched Lexus,
A homeless Vet pretends he's driving—
*Vroom-Vroom! Honk!*
The one caged-in tree on this pathetic cube of city-dirt is
Loitering for some bum to bum a smoke from, or spare change—

So many uncooperative initials—so many irregular hearts—carved in bus stop benches,
On city-trees, spray-painted on squatter buildings—so many suffocating bricks suffer
This incognito overpopulation of gouged out romance, love carelessly—yet carefully
Documented with a pocket knife while waiting for a city bus that's off schedule.

The intoxicated bus driver knocks over an entire row of mailboxes.
The tree is spared its stationary splintered humiliation.
For breakfast, carefully butter toast so the bread doesn't disintegrate.
It's a sad world; the broke yolk will never chicken up. So,

I patronized the coin operated Laundromat & opened a stranger's spinning dryer,
Stripped, threw my second hand stuff in & stole a slightly damp wardrobe.
I chewed gum & even blew bubbles during my escape.
I shave most days but didn't that day. Every day

I examine my chest hairs for deer ticks after my weak shower. I comb my head
For lice but need drugstore reading glasses; the things that infest us are so tiny,
Secretive. I see a dot of a man walking on a rooftop, peeping into any window without
Blinds, like a sniper with a telescopic lens & a high powered rifle but no actual bullets.

Most normal people don't get through life without a few trips to the emergency room—
Most normal people don't get through life

Without a broken bone or two, a few stitches; under chins is statistically
The most common scar.


An antagonistic wind plays 52 Pick-Up with a pile of recently raked leaves.
A tiny frog imprint
From a tiny frog trapped in wet cement is as permanent as it gets.
Hearts & initials are finger-drawn there too. Occasionally you see two entire names


Inside a sloppy heart. This is a world that really doesn't preserve too many new fossils.
The delivery guy double-parks then drives over the small patch of brown grass—
Backs into one of the few remaining mailboxes.
Taking a switchblade to my neighbor's wind chimes was my only real crime.


From the backseat I noticed the moon followed me home disguised in its jailbreak
Stolen-guard-uniform. I filed & re-filed a restraining order against the moon;
It's been stalking me my entire life.
If you catch people in the right frame of mind you can talk them into virtually anything.


I miss the old days, door-to-door encyclopedia salesmen & paperboys
Who rode bicycles with no hands & foot brakes & baseball cards in their spokes.
I once captured a bumble bee inside my fist so I wouldn't crush it.
Now, women barely look up in Laundromats or bus stations.
While mowing his tiny cube of lawn a man mangles his least significant toe.


The caged-in trees snicker in chorus, of course, because
Trees are paralyzed by their own wicked ideas:
Imaginative ones still levitate:
Imaginative ones refuse to shed their leaves or shed their leaves in summer
Just to be contrary. But most are rooted in their solid depression, like us.

# Implied Color

According to squirrel-behavior
It's going to be a bitch of a winter.
Barely October & blue collar
Squirrels already zippy
On Crystal Meth, acorns so scarce
They only appear on the black market.
So many of the people I love die

In October, the 20th to be exact.
Just yesterday I commiserated
With my one remaining friend
That even a hollow man requires six
Compatriots to carry his coffin.
Neither of us could even name two

Who would attend our funerals—
& though we joked with bravado,
We were both secretly horrified.
I'll carry you myself my friend said.
But what if you die first I said; I'm
Much weaker than you. I know, he said.
You can circle the street corner in the ghetto

& recruit illegal men who huddle in the chilly
Dawn praying for a day's labor, an honest
Life, cash under the table, a little dignity.
In Spain, pal, they hire professional mourners.
We will probably need them as well & audition
Temporary family members who'll wail

At designated cues in the eulogy.

Even the minister will have to fabricate

Our imaginary accomplishments,

Make our mundane sound like accolades,

Praise our pathetic masquerade on Earth

As though it meant something to somebody

Other than our selfish, hoarding selves.

# Conquering Your Acne

God intends us to come to our own feeble conclusions,
Like discovering a red hair in your Crème Brulee
At a chi-chi nightspot. You *could* discreetly signal a busboy.

You're tempted to storm out without paying.
Nobody caters to you anyway so saying nothing
Is no longer a viable option and all the perfectly postured

Ladies smell like the week-end.
You were hoping it would turn out differently;
You composed your Will, recited it actually

To the attorneys. So many of your personal prizes,
Original uncirculated Happy Meal Toys,
Will go unclaimed, stashed forever in rented self-storage.

Some will be inspected, fondled, then put up
For auction on eBay. You informed your closest friends,
Some of whom would be dead then, that the affair

Would begin at 8 sharp. Nobody eats before 8
In the city. Men standing in the bar three deep
Keep tabs on their time pieces. Growing old was not one

Of the multiple choices. So, you were not given even partial
Credit on that question. Now let me take a look at you.
*I can still see the little boy in you.*

Didn't you collect pristine 45's and preserve them in plastic?
Where are they now? Didn't seasons bleed into one another
Like watercolors in a kindergarten painting thumb-tacked to a bulletin board?

*It's me* you insisted! God excused himself to the public restroom
But never returned, apparently escaping through that tiny window.
There is no other logical explanation.

His single malt with a splash of soda sits on the table untouched.
The ice cube melting. The bargirl pities you—pity, pity, pity—
Takes your forgotten doggie bag to the alley and calls out

Here kitty! Here kitty, kitty, kitty...
Your father fought in the Golden Gloves as a flyweight for the city.
Posed photos of him in a weathered album is your inheritance,

Clenched fists without gloves, skinny legs and pale-pale skin.
Do you mind walking instead of taking a cab tonight?
It looks like the rain's stopping and the infomercial

On the bar TV is brokering a new miracle cure
As the week-end woman who noticed you has locked
Her pocketbook in the trunk of her new boyfriend's vehicle.

# Double Check

Be carefully reckless, not recklessly careful: make sure
Most street drugs you ingest are analyzed by professionals

But don't peddle your own prescriptions on the street.
The 24-hour donut shop does not even have a door lock.

If you have ever ripped a donut into a million pieces
You have some sense of how fractured your mind can be.

Each man is coded with prehistoric DNA that ignites
A force field against everyone entering his thoughts.

A more modern disguise: when your face is lathered
In shaving cream you are an insane naked man storming

His house accusing everyone of stealing his good razor.
Go put some clothes on your wife barks. It's an amazing

World. You can sprinkle hot-magic crystals on any icy
Driveway & putt-putt off to the job with no problem.

You can open your oven door & meat is evolving nicely
& appropriately sizzling. Most days, without even thinking

You take one step in front of the other & if your shoes
Are properly tied you won't trip. During any of the

Agonizing 24 hours someone's babbling on the tube:
Bad news can reach the speed of light or crack the sound

Barrier while poetry lollygags, shuffles back into the house
For something it forgot, or just to make sure the oven is off.

# Refrigerator Magnets

Children should aspire to rearrange
Their alphabets in revolutionary order,

Like a cache of counterfeit letters
Stashed in a deserted playground.

Abandoned refrigerators, left out
On curbs on trash nights,

Whose doors are still hinged
(Suffocate milk carton children).

The original shipping boxes were
The Time Machines they played

In when their existential existence
Fit so perfectly in breathing

Cardboard, more curious than any
Toy, more intoxicating than the fresh

Narcotic purple whiff of mimeograph
Before it was passed back to

The girl who spoke sparingly, whose
Name was alphabetically next.

# Anthropology

Young men are wired to overpopulate the world—
Murder everything in their paths they can't impregnate.

An ocean forms, the tide goes renegade. Knowledge
Is a raspberry bramble that sends underground runners

Once unnamed birds get tipsy on fermented berries,
Migration originally an offshoot of intuitive desire.

By the fifth season bushes sprout in unexpected places.
Even humans grow confused by the mysteries of hibernation—

Under appreciate laziness as a civilization. Remember
When bears & rice were still wild, all that was unnatural,

Natural, & vice versa? Once a human discovers an edible
Berry he hordes berries & all nature abandons him. Man has

Difficulty perceiving— witnesses only a shy haiku of his inner
Darkness, confuses beginnings with ends, is doubtful starts or

Completions exist, but recognizes birth & death. This is the
Motherfucker of contradictions children can't wrap their DNA

Around. The personal shields us from knowing. Knowing
Camouflages curiosity. Yet the sin against nature is to promote

The original while not recognizing the patterns of flora & stars.
Better to say nothing. Better to mold hope into a world that has no

Dimension or foreseeable outcome. The redundant waves turn wild,
Arbitrary, as that one disloyal microbe leans toward becoming, in

Its most primitive & pure form, neither feral nor random, but civilized—
Which is not a stagnation of customs, but adaptability to the great whim.

# Club X.T.C.

The assistant-manager raps-knocks-bangs on the strippers' dressing room door & inquires
If anyone is indecent, if everyone is decent.

I indentured myself to be an abstract con artist, apprenticing with invisibility—
Carrying my empty briefcase

To buildings that didn't exist. I wore near & far sighted contacts with x-ray lenses.
Not the comic book kind—

Flesh not skeletons intrigued me.
My wardrobe consisted of urgency & I resided mostly on the clock-side

Of the universe, listening to the B-sides, catching second-run discount matinees,
Making a bee-line to where trees diversify their portfolios of foliage—

It's a trick—a scam, a bait & switch, the seasons deceive us into thinking
The world is cyclical—not linear—no replacement leaf is identical to its predecessor.

An impersonator, an infiltrator, constantly slips in the backstage door
Past burly bouncers who barter for innovative drugs & freebies from strippers

Who posses double-jointed thumbs & religiously check their touch-screens
For fresh text messages. All I want is a girl in the flesh who signals

In complex eyelashes & stutters in linguistic sighs. There are blue skies somewhere,
But in this club no windows, or windows taped up with black construction paper.

Carpet patterns are busy-dingy & the light is so oxygen-depleted if you dropped your car
Keys you'd probably never find them—

# Half-Life

Autographed urine-colored snapshots of bit-character movie stars
In 50's pompadours camouflage the walls of Anthony's pizza parlor.


The fixture couple at their regular booth communicates with animated hand
Gestures; you've never been able to put two plus two together & Tony doesn't sell slices.


You should be committed to keeping pies whole, not half-baked, half-cocked,
Half-hearted, half-truths. Phone numbers of the recently dead exponentially


Multiply in your Rolodex. Hits on the jukebox remain time warped when
Tattoos meant you were a drunk & weeping Nebraska farm boy stationed


In a South Pacific jungle prison. Come home—no one will ever card you again;
Metal bars are starting to appear on ground floor apartment windows in your city.


Riffling medicine cabinets, a Roy G. Biv of pills, like exploding dice, in your sparrow
Nest hands. Swallow two reds, gulp a couple of Robin-egg-blues, slosh 'em down


With Black Label. Automobile air conditioners have not been invented
Yet so you kick out the passenger side window with scuffed Oxford loafers.


Secretly learning Italian, you exchange dollars for lire behind your shades.
It is never a simple conversion; one for one is not necessarily considered equal.


Even the moon's only half of its former self, as if a partial eclipse proved
The differentiation between being half-asleep or half-awake. Clocks jump


Ahead at 2 a.m. when people are less likely to make a fuss, wrapped up in their
Own nightmares. Divide the pie, but give your lover—always—the bigger half.

# Naïve Realism

Sidebar: the worst trouble is trouble-imagined.

Even though I am only one person

I'm turning into that talkative couple

Who always sits behind me at the movies:

Silent film did evolve into Talkies.


Being both participant and non-participant in life

Has its benefits, drawbacks, just as internal

And external governments exist we resist or resign

Ourselves to. We're bulimic gluttons, a smorgasbord

Of life-controls, ravenous for what's not available


Though we are all not-so-secret cannibals.

I've witnessed human beings exfoliate then evaporate

If when they don't succumb to their addictions slash

Desires to, say, bubble-wrap dancing, or deep frying

Their neighbor's pets. Sidebar: the secret President


Of these Un-united States is a bookie named Morton.

Most of our lives are on the fritz, like snowy televisions,

More expensive to fix than buy new.

I've seen modern cities under water, entire kitchens

River-floating, subways choir-less in their rumblings


When I miss my train; at those moments each of us is

A sort of bankrupt human bank: how can we envy the past

While slurping ice cream dots of the future?

The five o-clock whistle ignites the car-honking-season

Into vehicular stagnation, locking my keys in the running car

I abandon in that bumper traffic. As humans, we'd benefit

From more theme-parties: foot traffic is only dangerous if
We're trampled to death, otherwise, the clomping of shoes
Makes us feel world-included. Duck into the deli for a quick
Snack. Shoplift something tiny. Drink Holy water, but fruit

Flavored no-calorie-carbonated. Life-surprise is somewhat
Redundant so raise your hand if you consume too much think-time.
Even stray dogs bark with pictographic silence.
Without life-controls: dull job, evaporating and bottomless
Governments, cardboard spouses, rage grows exponentially

Till it depletes our human offshore bank account.
Without them, what monsters we'd become, wagering
Our souls to be un-cluded when dying is still life-unimagined.
Sidebar: Morton has determined the betting line, the spread,
The under-over, and we're all hopeless underdogs.

No one is favored. *Please.* You had to at least have had
A hunch The Prez was a sort of Pez dispenser.
Still, you pay the vig win or lose and each overtime game
Ultimately is played out to sudden death, sudden-life
In this topsy-turvy world where trouble is trouble-imagined.

# Re-Fresh

Barely—how barely I barely comprehend the particular particles of myself—

I mean to have meaningful conversations

But change slips through a hole in my pocket.

No, not *that* change. The big change.

An autistic lifetime undiagnosed, I rip labels from the collars of my dress shirts—

I don't wish to be reminded of methodical shrinking, or the slow torture

Of a thousand tiny paper cuts, or my dead father breathing down my neckline.

They are—these shirts—colors everyone debates—

That's a shy turquoise not grey—no, it's a newly discovered shade of jade.

Evidence we see the world through our own eyes is in every argument, huh?

Religiously I answer my landline to mechanical pre-recorded solicitors.

Back-talk and wisecracks to machines is never satisfying.

My wife contends televisions

Of the future will be invisible pieces of furniture

And we'll view holograms of our fantasies instead—

Beats huddling around a wooden radio trying to clean up

The static with clockwise twists of rabbit ear antennas I reckon.

I am oh so clever with my affirmative responses

But my face lately voluntarily

Goes side-to-side like the collective head-movement

Of drag race spectators, even though I studied to be a sort of bobble head.

Hair nets are losing their popularity

Except with immigrant restaurant workers but based

Upon demographics the uneducated will be the majority soon.

A guy sporting a hair net could someday be President!

I am of a certain age where it's becoming less reliable

To drive at night but I hope to refinance my blind spots

With an adjustable: I plan to get out of life before the rates jump.

Contemplating the lack of meaning, I am any redundant man

Who lives alone with his television and predictable take-out,

Who's rousted from his bed in the drizzly dark in his frayed bathrobe

Watching his flop house go up in flames from the over-wiring of archaic

Appliances. The moon has been lobbying for centuries for its spin

On the swing shift. Sirens seem to come from every direction

Or one doesn't fully appreciate from which direction they are coming.

Next morning, obviously, the dwelling no longer exists

But long-time residents still possess keys to their self-installed deadbolts

And recite their non-existent addresses to Red Cross volunteers and cops.

In their ratty way, rats comb the rat classifieds for new apartments.

When the ambulance pulls up, everyone wonders who it is for.

# Rummaging

Here is the paint-by-numbers painting of Sitting Bull's pony she painted.
Here is her imitation Navajo loom she used to weave turquoise blankets.
Here is her afternoon martini shaker and the prescription Black Beauties.
Mahjong tiles click rhythmically by arthritic hands of her bilingual generation.

Outside the rain rains sideways, horizontal as this world is, forcing umbrellas
Inside-out, causing even the sun to go insane. The rush-hour train stops
At every unpronounceable station; there's no express to her town anymore;
Her beauty parlor hair no longer appears regularly, clogging the shower drain.

Seasons have turned profoundly unseasonal, commercials for funeral homes
Hum effluvium as white background noise; when you need one it's a quick
Flip through the yellow pages with a kind of all-you-can-eat attitude,
A connect-the-dots Dadaism. The dial on the radio circles counterclockwise,

Continuously, stuck on a station from the Big Band era, squeaky pitched
Static only Guy Lambardo hears. How hard it is to follow her life's bouncing ball
Out the asylum's third storey, ignoring her most personal curfews, escaping
On trains one hears but never sees, diaries composed in disappearing ink.

Grateful acknowledgement is made to the editors of the following
periodicals who were kind enough to publish these poems.

| | |
|---|---|
| *AGNI Online*: | "Unofficial Life" |
| *Barnstorm*: | "Rage" |
| *Cimarron Review*: | "Naïve Realism" |
| *Cold Mountain Review*: | "Double Check" |
| *The Collagist*: | "Implied Color" |
| *Diode*: | "Now Baby or Never" |
| | "The Good Ship Lollipop" |
| *Drunken Boat*: | "Dumping on the Bartender at the Pussy Cat Lounge" |
| | "Straddling the World" |
| *Green Mountains Review*: | "To a Girl Walking By a Construction Site Ignoring the Catcalls & Wolf-Whistles" |
| *The Literary Review*: | "A Rare Condition" |
| | "Art Therapy" |
| | "Divine Wow:" |
| *Missouri Review Online*: | "The World Haywire" |
| *PANK*: | "Rediscovering Gravity" |
| *Ploughshares*: | "Rummaging" |

|                            |                                |
|---------------------------:|--------------------------------|
| *Poet Lore*:               | "Bus Tokens"                   |
| *Scythe*:                  | "Winter Escape Artist"         |
|                            | "Anthropology"                 |
|                            | "Club X.T.C"                   |
|                            | "Refrigerator Magnets"         |
|                            | "Re-Fresh"                     |
| *Southern Humanities Review*: | "Brown Bagging It"          |
| *Southern Review*:         | "Dead Telegram to a Dead Poet" |
| *Superstition Review*:     | "The Czar of Hartford"         |
|                            | "Convivial Pleasures"          |
| *Tuesday; An Art Project*: | "Cooking With Deception"       |
| *Western Humanities Review*: | "Conquering Your Acne"       |
| *Zocalo Public Square*:    | "Half-Life"                    |

"Divine Wow" also appeared on *Verse Daily*, March 31st 2010
"Dead Telegram for a Dead Poet" also appeared on *Verse Daily*, May 27th 2010

*Renee Ashley & Alan Michael Parker were kind enough to read this*
*manuscript in an earlier form and offered helpful suggestions.*
*Big thanks to the Splinta Group: Ellen, Leslie, Pam, T.C. & Wally.*

Bruce Cohen's poems have appeared in many literary periodicals such as *AGNI*, *The Georgia Review*, *The Harvard Review*, *Ploughshares*, *Poetry* and *The Southern Review*. They have also been featured on *Poetry Daily* and *Verse Daily*. He has published two previous books: *Disloyal Yo-Yo* (Dream Horse Press), which was awarded the 2007 Orphic Poetry Prize, and *Swerve* (Black Lawrence Press). A recipient of an artist grant from the Connecticut Commission on Culture & Tourism, he currently teaches poetry and creative writing at the University of Connecticut.